I0796009

My First Pet

Lizards

by Vanessa Black

Bullfrog Books

Ideas for Parents and Teachers

Bullfrog Books let children practice reading informational text at the earliest reading levels. Repetition, familiar words, and photo labels support early readers.

Before Reading

- Discuss the cover photo. What does it tell them?
- Look at the picture glossary together. Read and discuss the words.

Read the Book

- "Walk" through the book and look at the photos. Let the child ask questions. Point out the photo labels.
- Read the book to the child, or have him or her read independently.

After Reading

- Prompt the child to think more. Ask: What do you need to take care of a lizard? Would you like one as a pet?

Bullfrog Books are published by Jump!
5357 Penn Avenue South
Minneapolis, MN 55419
www.jumplibrary.com

Copyright © 2017 Jump! International copyright reserved in all countries. No part of this book may be reproduced in any form without written permission from the publisher.

Library of Congress Cataloging-in-Publication Data

Names: Black, Vanessa, author.
Title: Lizards / by Vanessa Black.
Description: Minneapolis, MN: Jump!, Inc., [2017]
Series: My first pet | Audience: Age 5–8.
Audience: Grade K to grade 3.
Includes bibliographical references and index.
Identifiers: LCCN 2016027485 (print)
LCCN 2016028433 (ebook)
ISBN 9781620315538 (hardcover: alk. paper)
ISBN 9781624965012 (ebook)
Subjects: LCSH: Lizards—Juvenile literature.
Classification: LCC QL666.L2 B58 2017 (print)
LCC QL666.L2 (ebook) | DDC 597.95—dc23
LC record available at https://lccn.loc.gov/2016027485

Editor: Kirsten Chang
Book Designer: Michelle Sonnek
Photo Researcher: Michelle Sonnek

Photo Credits: All photos by Shutterstock except: Age Fotostock, 8, 23br; Alamy, 10–11, 14, 23bl; Getty, 5, 6–7, 18–19, 23mr; iStock, 20–21; Superstock, 1, 16–17, 23tl.

Printed in the United States of America at Corporate Graphics in North Mankato, Minnesota.

Table of Contents

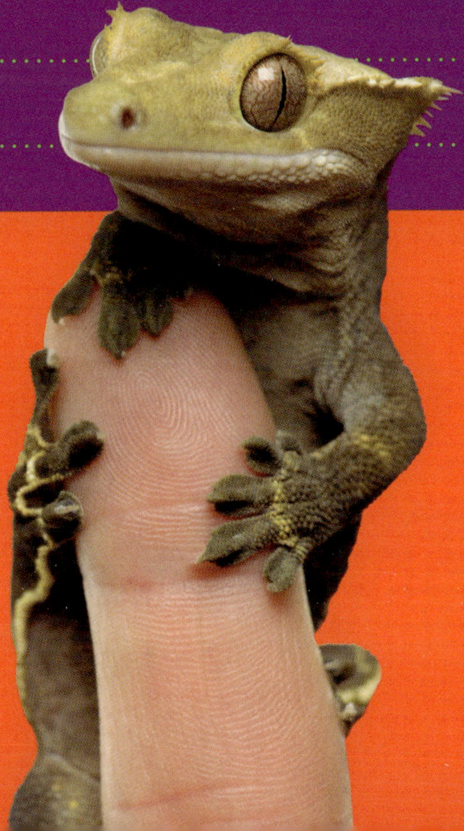

A New Pet

Nils wants a lizard.

There are many kinds of lizards.

What are they all like?
He asks his friends.

Mel has a tegu.
Bella is big!

She is longer than Mel's cat.
She needs a large tank.

leash

Mel can walk
her on a leash.

Nico is Asa's crested gecko.

He is small.

He likes to hide.

Gary has a bearded dragon.

Mo is a quiet pet.

He likes to be held.

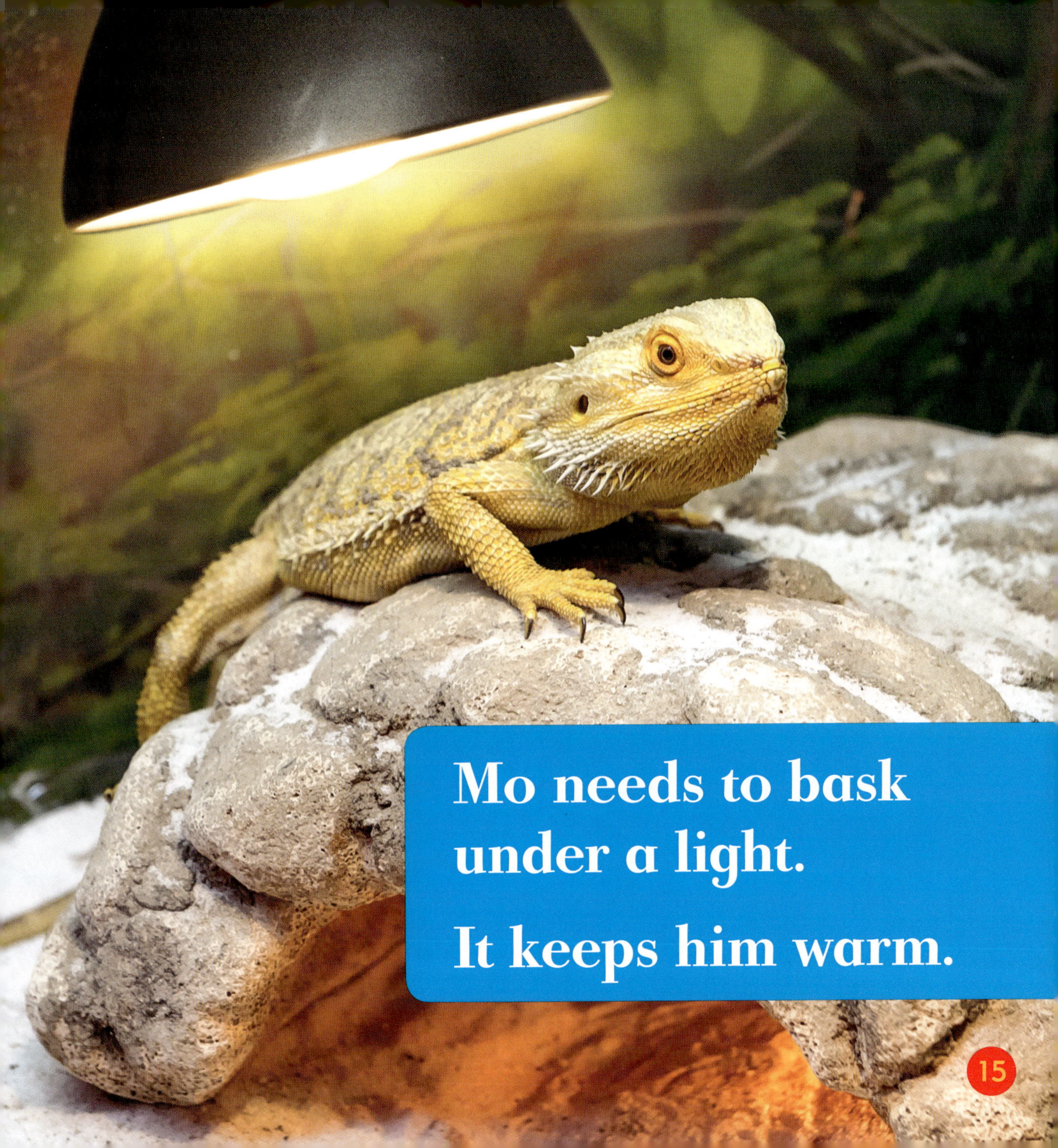

Mo needs to bask under a light.

It keeps him warm.

Kim has an ackie.
His name is Gorn.
He eats crickets.

What kind of lizard does Nils get?

A leopard gecko.

They live a long time.

Jax could live
to be 20 years old!